I0012141

Jordan Blake

SEO Mastery

Dedication by Jordan Blake:

To the relentless pursuers of online excellence,

May your digital endeavors be guided by the wisdom within these pages. This work is dedicated to those who strive for visibility, innovate in obscurity, and master the ever-shifting dance of SEO.

Jordan Blake

Epigraph by Jordan Blake:

"In the symphony of search, every keystroke is a note, every link a chord. Navigate the algorithms with purpose, for in the realm of SEO, your website's melody echoes in the chambers of digital prominence."

—

Jordan   Blake

Contents

9.

10.

11.

12.

Foreword

Foreword by Jordan Blake:

In the vast digital expanse where every click echoes in the algorithms of search engines, mastering the art of SEO is akin to wielding a digital scepter. As we delve into the pages of "SEO Mastery Unveiled," I invite you to embark on a transformative journey—one that transcends the conventional and catapults you into the echelons of online prominence.

The world of SEO is a living, breathing entity, and within these chapters, you'll find not just techniques, but a philosophy—a philosophy that places your website at the nexus of visibility and relevance. From the strategic dance of keywords to the symphony of social signals, each strategy is a brushstroke in the masterpiece of online success.

As we navigate the ever-shifting tides of digital dynamics, remember that SEO is not merely a set of tactics; it's a mindset—an understanding of the intricate dance between content, user experience, and the algorithms that govern our digital universe.

So, dear reader, fasten your seatbelt as we embark on this exhilarating journey. "SEO Mastery Unveiled" is not just a guide; it's your compass in the uncharted territories of online visibility. Let the mastery begin.

Jordan   Blake

Preface

Preface by Jordan Blake:

Welcome to the dynamic realm of SEO mastery! In this ever-evolving digital landscape, understanding the intricacies of search engine optimization is not just a skill; it's a strategic advantage. As someone deeply immersed in the world of online visibility and digital excellence, I'm thrilled to guide you through the nuances of SEO.

In "SEO Mastery Unveiled," we embark on a journey to unravel the core strategies that can transform your website's visibility. From the art of keyword alchemy to the orchestration of social signals, each chapter is a gateway to unlocking your website's true potential.

These pages are not just a guide; they are a roadmap to navigate the intricate algorithms and ever-shifting trends that define the digital frontier. Whether you're a seasoned marketer or a curious entrepreneur, the insights within will empower you to harness the power of SEO in 2023 and beyond.

So, let's dive into the world of SEO mastery, where the digital possibilities are limitless, and your website's ascent to prominence begins. Here's to elevating your online presence and embracing the transformative journey ahead.

Jordan   Blake

Acknowledgement

Acknowledgments by Jordan Blake:

In the symphony of digital exploration, no endeavor is truly solitary. As I stand on the precipice of "SEO Mastery Unveiled," I am compelled to express my gratitude to those who have illuminated my path and fueled this odyssey.

To the tireless architects of knowledge, the SEO maestros who continue to shape the landscape, your insights are the foundation upon which this work stands. Your dedication to unraveling the intricacies of search engine optimization has been a beacon of inspiration.

To the unsung heroes behind the scenes—designers, editors, and collaborators—your craftsmanship has transformed words into an immersive journey. Your commitment to excellence has shaped each page, creating a tapestry of wisdom.

To the readers and seekers of digital enlightenment, this endeavor is for you. Your curiosity fuels the perpetual evolution of this field, and it is your quest for mastery that breathes life into the very essence of "SEO Mastery Unveiled."

May this exploration serve as a testament to the collaborative spirit that propels us forward. In the vast expanse of digital discovery, let us continue to navigate, learn, and grow together.

With gratitude,

Jordan   Blake

1

Understanding the Basics of SEO:

U nderstanding the Basics of SEO:

SEO, or Search Engine Optimization, is the practice of enhancing your website's visibility on search engines. Start by familiarizing yourself with key concepts:

-Keywords: These are terms people use to search. Identify relevant keywords for your content.

- On-Page Optimization: Optimize your web pages by placing keywords in titles, headings, and meta descriptions.

- Backlinks: These are links from other websites to yours. Quality backlinks can boost your site's authority.

- User Experience: Ensure your site is easy to navigate and provides value to visitors.

-Content Quality:Create valuable, relevant, and well-structured content.

As you delve into SEO, keep these basics in mind for a solid foundation.

2

Keyword Research Mastery:

Keyword Research Mastery:

Keyword research is crucial for effective SEO. Here's a brief guide:

1. Start with a Seed List: Brainstorm and create a list of potential keywords related to your content or business.

2. Use Keyword Tools: Utilize tools like Google Keyword Planner, SEMrush, or Ahrefs to expand your list and find relevant keywords. Consider search volume and competition.

3. Long-Tail Keywords: Include specific, longer phrases that users might search for. These can be less competitive and more targeted.

4. Competitor Analysis: Analyze competitors' keywords. Identify gaps or opportunities in your strategy.

5. User Intent: Understand the intent behind the search. Create content that aligns with what users are looking for.

6. Refine and Update: Regularly revisit and update your keyword strategy based on changing trends and your content focus.

By mastering keyword research, you'll optimize your content for what your audience is actively searching, enhancing your site's   visibility.

3

Creating High-Quality Content:

Creating High-Quality Content:

Crafting content that resonates with both users and search engines is essential for SEO success. Here's a concise guide:

1. Relevance is Key: Ensure your content is directly related to your target audience and addresses their needs or questions.

2. Quality Over Quantity: Prioritize creating valuable, well-researched content rather than focusing solely on the volume of material.

3. Engaging Headlines: Craft compelling headlines to grab attention and encourage users to click through.

4. Structure Matters: Organize your content with clear headings, subheadings, and paragraphs. Use bullet points and numbered lists for readability.

5. Keyword Placement: Incorporate relevant keywords naturally within your content. Avoid keyword stuffing, as it can harm your SEO.

6. Multimedia Elements: Enhance your content with images, videos, and other multimedia elements to make it more engaging.

7. Regular Updates: Keep your content current and relevant. Periodically update and refresh existing content to maintain its value.

8. User Experience: Prioritize a positive user experience. Fast loading times and mobile-friendliness contribute to user satisfaction.

By focusing on these aspects, you'll create content that not only appeals to your audience but also aligns with search engine algorithms, improving your SEO performance.

4

On-Page Optimization Techniques:

O n-Page Optimization Techniques:

On-page optimization involves fine-tuning individual web pages to improve their visibility and relevance for search engines. Here's a concise guide:

1. Title Tags: Craft unique and compelling title tags for each page, incorporating relevant keywords. Keep them concise and under 60 characters.

2. Meta Descriptions:Write informative meta descriptions that summarize the page content. Include a call-to-action and stay within 155-160 characters.

3. Header Tags (H1, H2, etc.): Use header tags to structure your content. The H1 tag represents the main heading and should contain your primary keyword.

4. URL Structure: Create SEO-friendly URLs that are concise, descriptive, and include keywords where relevant.

5. Keyword Placement: Strategically place keywords in the content, headers, and meta tags. Ensure it feels natural and doesn't disrupt readability.

6. Image Alt Text: Include descriptive alt text for images, incorporating relevant keywords. This not only aids accessibility but also provides additional context for search engines.

7. Internal Linking: Link to other relevant pages within your website. This helps distribute link equity and guides users to related content.

8. Optimized Content: Ensure your content is well-written, informative, and adds value to the user. Address the user's query comprehensively.

By implementing these on-page optimization techniques, you enhance your page's visibility and relevance in search engine results.

5

Mobile Optimization Basics:

Mobile Optimization Basics:

As more users access the internet on mobile devices, optimizing your website for mobile is crucial. Here's a brief guide:

1. Responsive Design: Ensure your website design adapts to various screen sizes. Responsive design provides a seamless user experience across devices.

2. Page Speed: Optimize loading times for mobile users. Compress images, minimize redirects, and leverage browser caching to enhance speed.

3. Mobile-Friendly Content: Create content that is easily readable on smaller screens. Use concise paragraphs, legible fonts, and appropriately-sized buttons.

4. Viewport Configuration: Set the viewport meta tag to ensure your site displays correctly on mobile devices, adjusting to the device's width.

5. Avoid Flash: Flash content may not be supported on many mobile devices. Use HTML5 and CSS3 for animations and interactivity.

6. Mobile-Friendly Navigation: Simplify navigation for mobile users. Use a clear and concise menu, and consider mobile-friendly navigation patterns.

7. Testing: Regularly test your website on various mobile devices to identify and fix any issues. Google's Mobile-Friendly Test can help evaluate your site's mobile optimization.

By prioritizing mobile optimization, you enhance user experience, which is a significant factor in search engine rankings.

6

Building a Quality Backlink Profile:

Building a Quality Backlink Profile:

Backlinks, or links from other websites to yours, play a vital role in SEO. Here's a brief guide on building a strong backlink profile:

1. Quality Over Quantity: Focus on obtaining links from authoritative and relevant websites rather than pursuing a large number of low-quality links.

2. Relevance Matters: Seek backlinks from websites that are related to your industry or niche. Relevance adds credibility to your site.

3. Natural Link Building:Aim for organic links by creating high-quality content that others want to reference and share. Shareable content attracts backlinks naturally.

4. Guest Posting: Contribute guest posts to reputable websites in your industry. Ensure your guest content provides value and includes a link back to your site.

5. Broken Link Building:bIdentify broken links on other websites, and offer your content as a replacement. This is a win-win strategy for both parties.

6. Social Media Promotion: Share your content on social media platforms to increase its visibility. While social signals themselves may not directly impact SEO, social sharing can lead to more backlink opportunities.

7. Monitor Your Profile: Regularly check your backlink profile using tools like Google Search Console or third-party tools. Disavow any harmful or spammy links.

8.Collaborate with Influencers: Partner with influencers or thought leaders in your industry. Their endorsement can result in valuable backlinks.

By focusing on quality, relevance, and diverse sources, you'll build a backlink profile that enhances your site's authority and SEO performance.

7

Prioritizing User Experience for SEO:

P rioritizing User Experience for SEO:

Creating a positive user experience on your website is not only essential for visitors but also influences search engine rankings. Here's a concise guide:

1. Page Loading Speed: Optimize your website's loading speed. Users and search engines favor fast-loading pages. Compress images, use browser caching, and minimize unnecessary elements.

2. Mobile-Friendly Design: Ensure your website is responsive and provides a seamless experience across various devices. Google prioritizes mobile-friendly sites in its rankings.

3. Intuitive Navigation: Design a clear and intuitive navigation structure. Users should easily find the information they're looking for without confusion.

4.Readable Content: Use legible fonts, appropriate font sizes, and maintain a good contrast between text and background. Break content into digestible sections with headers and bullet points.

5. Minimize Pop-Ups: While pop-ups can be effective, use them sparingly. Intrusive pop-ups can disrupt the user experience and affect SEO.

6. Clear Call-to-Action (CTA): Guide users on what actions to take with clear and strategically placed calls-to-action. This can improve engagement and conversions.

7. Secure Website (HTTPS):Ensure your website has a secure connection (HTTPS). This not only builds trust but is also a ranking factor for Google.

8. Regular Updates: Keep your website content and design up-to-date. An outdated website may deter users and impact search engine rankings.

By prioritizing user experience, you enhance your website's appeal to visitors and align with search engine algorithms, contributing to improved SEO performance.

8

Mastering Analytics for SEO:

Mastering Analytics for SEO:

Understanding and utilizing analytics tools is crucial for optimizing your website's performance. Here's a brief guide:

1. Google Analytics Setup: Install Google Analytics to track website traffic, user behavior, and other valuable metrics. Set up relevant goals to measure conversions.

2. Traffic Sources: Analyze where your website traffic is coming from – whether it's organic search, social media, referrals, or direct visits. Focus on channels that bring in quality traffic.

3. User Behavior: Examine user interactions on your site. Identify popular pages, high bounce rates, and user flow. Adjust your content and design based on these insights.

4. Conversion Tracking: Define and track conversions that align with your business goals. This could be form submissions, product purchases, or other desired actions.

5. Keyword Performance: Use tools to monitor keyword performance. Identify high-performing keywords and areas for improvement. Adjust your content strategy accordingly.

6. Page Speed Analysis: Check your website's loading times and address any issues. Slow-loading pages can lead to higher bounce rates.

7. Mobile Analytics: Evaluate mobile-specific metrics to ensure a seamless mobile experience. This includes mobile bounce rates, popular devices, and user engagement on mobile platforms.

8. Competitor Analysis: Use analytics tools to gain insights into your competitors. Identify their strengths and weaknesses to refine your own strategy.

By regularly reviewing analytics data, you can make informed decisions to optimize your website, improve user experience, and enhance your overall SEO strategy.

9

Staying Updated in the Dynamic World of SEO:

Staying Updated in the Dynamic World of SEO:

SEO is an ever-evolving field, and staying informed about the latest trends and updates is crucial. Here's a brief guide:

1. Follow Industry Blogs:Regularly read reputable SEO blogs and websites. They often provide insights into algorithm updates, industry trends, and best practices.

2. Search Engine Guidelines: Stay abreast of search engine guidelines, especially updates from major search engines like Google. Understanding their recommendations can help you align your strategy with their goals.

3.Attend Webinars and Conferences: Participate in webinars and attend SEO conferences. These events offer opportunities to learn from experts, gain new perspectives, and network with other professionals.

4. Online Courses: Enroll in online courses to deepen your SEO knowledge. Platforms like Moz, SEMrush, and HubSpot offer comprehensive courses on SEO.

5. Join SEO Communities: Engage with SEO communities on forums and social media platforms. Discussing ideas and challenges with peers can provide valuable insights.

6. Experiment and Test: Conduct your own experiments and A/B tests. This hands-on approach can help you understand how changes impact your website's performance.

7. Subscribe to Newsletters: Subscribe to newsletters from trusted SEO sources. Receive regular updates and summaries of important developments in the SEO world.

8. Google Algorithm Updates: Keep an eye on major Google algorithm updates. Understanding these changes can help you adapt your strategy to maintain or improve your search rankings.

By staying proactive and continuously educating yourself, you'll be better equipped to navigate the dynamic landscape of SEO and implement strategies that align with the latest industry standards.

10

Integrating Social Media for SEO:

Integrating Social Media for SEO:

Social media can indirectly impact your SEO efforts. Here's a brief guide on leveraging social platforms:

1. Content Sharing: Share your website content on social media platforms. Engaging content that gets shared may indirectly contribute to increased visibility and backlinks.

2. Build a Following: Grow your social media following. A larger audience can lead to more social shares, potentially expanding your content's reach.

3. Engagement Matters: Actively engage with your audience on social media. Respond to comments, encourage discussions, and foster a community around your brand.

4. Optimized Profiles: Optimize your social media profiles with accurate information, a link to your website, and relevant keywords. This can enhance your brand's online presence.

5. Social Signals: While the direct impact of social signals on SEO is debated, a strong social presence can positively influence your brand's reputation and indirectly contribute to search engine rankings.

6. Use Hashtags Strategically: Utilize relevant hashtags to increase the discoverability of your content on platforms like Twitter and Instagram.

7. Visual Content: Incorporate visually appealing content. Images and videos tend to perform well on social media, increasing the likelihood of engagement and shares.

8. Promote Events and Content: Share information about events, promotions, and new content on your website through social media channels to generate interest and traffic.

By integrating social media into your overall SEO strategy, you can enhance brand visibility, engage with your audience, and potentially drive more traffic to your website.

www.ingramcontent.com/pod-product-compliance
Lightning Source LLC
LaVergne TN
LVHW051633050326
832903LV00033B/4730